Reco

Voices

Edited by
Helen Aitchison

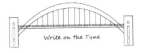

Write on the Tyne Publishing

To anyone who has been impacted by addiction.

We offer strength to those that have survived, those trying to survive, and compassion for those we have lost.

Contents

Foreword

Recovery Connections is based in Middlesbrough but works in communities across the North East of England. Led by the people we support and the communities we work alongside, this body of inspiring work was created amongst the more than one thousand people we support each year, and the ninety per cent lived experience staff we employ.

With more than three centuries of addiction recovery across our growing charity, through this culture of recovery, we coach, nurture, train, educate, inspire, and empower individuals and communities to achieve their full potential and for people to live their best lives.

This collection of experiences is one of the many ways we diversify in order to reach new people and audiences. It is through the sharing of stories that we raise awareness of recovery and challenge stigma. We also maintain a high street presence in the form of social enterprise businesses, provide consultancy and training packages for employee wellbeing programmes, and develop recovery access for students in universities across the UK.

For more than 15 years, the overarching aim of our innovative and entrepreneurial charity has been to break down barriers, create opportunities to share experiences, and to deepen an understanding of recovery, wherever we possibly can.

This is where the magic of recovery happens. This is the power of lived experience.

To find out more, please visit:
www.recoveryconnections.org.uk

Trigger warning – this book contains references to drug taking, alcohol misuse, sexual abuse, domestic violence, and suicide.

A Dream Dying

Anonymous

I had a dream that died,

When I picked up that needle,

My dream turned,

Into a nightmare.

A reoccurring nightmare,

Painful and frightening.

That I thought could only end,

Not from waking,

But when I could dream no more.

A nightmare that became reality,

I couldn't wake up from.

Existing in a life not worth living,

I wanted out of addiction.

I tried, and failed,

Time and time again.

On repeat, unable to change the record.

I danced with death,

Only one or two steps ahead,

As it crept up on me,

Caught my breath with an evil laugh.

Death tried to stand on my feet,

Stamp on my soul,

Disable me,

Dominate me.

Death nearly won.

I was on my knees,

Until I reached out for help,

As Death's door tried to trap me,

Closer, ensnared,

Threatening to lock me inside,

Forever.

I reached for help,

It offered a hand.

I grabbed,

Grasped, and wouldn't let go.

Recovery Connections,

They kept a hold of me,

And death lost its grip,

Forever.

Chaos in Motion

Andreas Theologou

Addiction is like sunflower roots,

Growing very deep.

Growing up,

Looking from the outside in,

Seeing the destruction and pain.

This monster,

Was meant to love,

But

     all

        it

           does

              is

                 scar.

Family in tatters.

Punishments not forthcoming.

Cover ups and hurt.

IGNORED,

By the possible shame of,

TRUTH.

How dare you leave those kids,

to cover up,

Your embarrassment.

Their hunger and bruises,

No longer remain.

But

      their

            hearts

                  forever

                        cracked.

They turned into beautiful beings,

Despite the abuse.

UNLIKE YOU.

A monster.

Wars and nightmares combined,

Would have been a walk in the park,

Compared to,

A day spent with you.

I'd advise you as a recovery worker,

To get the help you need.

But

    I

        know

           you.

The kids are alright.

You, my dear monster, are forgiven.

Born to destroy,

Knowing no better.

WE FORGIVE YOU.

My beautiful dog, Lily – a shining light

<u>A Letter to you, Dad</u>

J

Dear Dad,

I never acknowledged you as a man with wants and needs, just simply as Dad.

"Simply Dad."

Now I realise just how much you have done in your life and the term "simply Dad," is demoralising. You made life enjoyable. Always joking around, basically a mischievous little boy in a man's body!

It's no wonder people are attracted to you with your huge personality – always smiling and looking on the bright side of life.

Dad, you were always interested in the activities we did, even being the only dad watching me play hockey on a Saturday morning. Then we grew up, becoming adults ourselves and left home.

Along came grandkids and you bought a minibus to take them out.

The other kids in the street would fight over who would get the free seat after all the grandkids were accounted for!

Dad, you taught us right from wrong, how to be positive and enjoy life.

I lost that somewhere but it's coming back now.

As well as your family, you still had time for Mam and to pursue your own interests. You've built your home, you got your apartment in Greece, you restored the motorbikes and classic cars that you wanted. You prefer to be outside in the fresh air and hate the thought of sitting about the house.

You went to watch Sunderland play football and had your rock 'n' roll disco! Birds, walking, the list of your hobbies and goals is endless.

I know parents are supposed to say they are proud of their kids and I think you are. You still sing 'Here Come the Girls,' when we are together.

But Dad, I want to say to you that I am so proud and humbled to have you as my dad.

Thank you for everything that you have done for us all, across the years.

When I think of you I can't help but smile. You brighten up anyone's day.

Love,

J

xxx

Addiction

Anonymous

A lways focused on the next drink.

D estruction and damage caused in amounts I'd rather not think.

D arkness with no light at the end of the tunnel.

I don't need a glass, just give me a funnel.

C an't stop, won't stop,

T he insides of my body are ready to pop.

I n pain, going insane,

O n a pathway to a life extinguished,

N ow is the time to seek help.

Time

Annette Patton

As I sit all alone,

I've never felt so isolated,

In my own home.

Not knowing if it's day or night,

My mind is battling,

A constant fight.

I'm so scared,

Hearts racing,

Body's aching.

I wished just one person fucking cared.

My best friend,

Has become my glass,

Which I hardly let out my grasp.

Drinking wine,

A glass at a time.

Before I know it,

Onto glass number nine.

My life has become unmanageable,

In every single way.

I slump my head in my hands,

I cry, I scream, I pray.

Those awful demons,

Playing games in my head.

Keep whispering to me,

'Annette, you're better off dead.'

Trying to escape this awful disease,

I trip,

I slip,

I fall to my knees.

As I lie slumped on my bed,

1001 negative thoughts,

Enter my head.

Wiping tears as I cry,

I look up to Lewis, my son,

Shouting 'Mam! Why the fuck, why?'

Lying, cheating, manipulating,

Was the name of the game.

I hang my head,

In the greatest shame.

My other son, Sean,

He saw it too.

'Mam, please get help, we love you.'

Lewis kept saying,

'You've got a problem, can't you see?'

But this problem they could see,

Wasn't visible to me.

The kids full of anger,

Rage and despair.

Turned around,

And flew down the stairs.

Lewis shouting,

'I'll get you help, I fucking care.'

The days turned into nights,

And the nights into days,

Everything in my life,

Becoming a haze.

My kids did their best,

Put me to the test.

Detox, rehab, and all the rest.

Six months in rehab has reprogrammed me,

If it wasn't for my Lewis,

Fuck knows where I'd be!

PROBABLY DEAD!

I owe my life to the both of you. Lewis (left) Sean (right).
You are my absolute world and I'm so blessed to have two
amazing sons,
Love always,
Mam
Xxx

The Jester and the Fool

Andreas Theologou

Part 1

The Fool,

I am the forgiver.

I see you and feel pain.

Hate or love,

I am unsure,

I fear to discover which it is.

Too much time has passed.

You care not of me.

Actions have shown,

It is time to cut these chains,

Made of false words,

It's time to live.

Shatter the memories and the heart,

With tears to mend both.

With time, destiny will bring me truth,

But time has shown,

And exposed the false.

With great realisation,

Has come great pain.

It's time for the crow to fly,

And leave me shattered.

Leave me to rebuild,

With peace and sanity.

The light doesn't shine,

Bright on me.

It will be long before it does.

Too many times has the pattern,

Given good to bad.

Not that I am a good,

Nor deserving of the good.

But you are a monster,

Pulling strings.

Mine and others alike.

I rid of you with great desire,

Betrayer.

Inspired by The Wheel of Time by Robert Jordan

A Reflection of Superheroes

Terry Ridley

A little boy has a passion, just to kick a football and play like his heroes.

Always going home full of mud and bruised shins, but always happy.

Getting his new boots, he would put his kit on, look into the mirror and see his football hero.

With a big smile and hope in his eyes, he looked past his reflection and saw happiness and love.

He can just be...

Life changes quick for our little boy.

Now a young man, feeling afraid and alone.

He wears a uniform and when he looks at his reflection he sees the hero he is expected to be, but in his eyes is the little boy who just wants to be...

His uniform has been taken away and a whole new world has opened up for our young man. A villain, who was a hero to our young man, eventually showed his true side and tried to break him. In his reflection he is battered and bruised with the fearful eyes of the little boy who

Just wants to be...

His reflection changes so much now, it's like he's watching 100 different movies, with him the bad guy in all of them. Now at rock bottom, body scared, heart broken, a real hero came along.

He looked him in the eyes, smiled and gave him a choice:

Come with me and we will support you. All I ask of you, is that you try.

Fast forward and life is good for our man.

He has a big smile, hope in his eyes, and love in his heart.

He is surrounded by heroes every day and that's why he has a reflection of superheroes.

Now he can just be...

Dear Future Me

Anonymous

Dear Future Me,

Some days you will struggle, it will never go away completely and you need to know that. But you will learn to adapt, to change, and to alter – you will get what you need to keep going. Friends, sponsors, support services will all be your new substance – a healthy, safe substance that doesn't destroy you and everything around you. But you can't rely on everyone for everything. You have to let them help you to walk but not walk for you. You have to regain responsibility, when you can.

Take control of your future.

But it won't be plain sailing, an easy ride. If it was, you wouldn't have failed to keep afloat all those times. Life is hard, addiction is hard. It's an illness, physically and mentally and you will have to keep working on it and keep aiming to be the best you that you can. No one can ask more of you, just try your best and don't make excuses.

Understand that you are human and will make mistakes, like you have in the past. You've made many mistakes but you are putting them right. You will keep putting them right and trying.

Be kind to yourself and people around you. You never know what's going on in a person's life so try not to judge. Life can be a struggle, you know that but we are fighters and we keep going.

So keep going, never give up and be proud of the steps you take, no matter how small.

With love,

Me

xxx

Forever Fly Free

Emma Day

Take my hand,

And follow me,

If you want a life,

That is beautiful and free.

On your journey,

Walk next to me.

I've been fortunate,

To be back in reality.

Step by step,

Day by day.

The storm will pass,

Go on its way.

Trust me please,

My storm passed!

The fear will go,

The rain won't last.

I know you can do this.

It's clear to see,

You have had enough,

A life of misery.

Walk through the darkness,

Into the sun.

Believe me when I say,

Life can be such fun.

I will be here to guide you,

Through the thick and thin.

This is a battle,

I know you can win.

A beautiful life,

Just in arms reach.

This is what I'm trying to teach.

You're a wonderful person,

Inside and out.

This battle you will win,

I have no doubt.

Take my hand and be with me.

This is your time to start recovery.

Listen to my voice,

So honest and true.

What reason do I have,

To lie to you?

Hear my words,

Caring and strong.

You'll be back on top,

Where you belong.

Time to be strong,

Please come along,

We can both sing together,

A victory song.

Jump on this band wagon,

Called recovery.

Together we will both have wings,

To forever fly free.

Dedicated to Recovery Connections

Better Days are Coming

Lisa Peacock

Will I ever get out of here?

A place full of darkness and pain.

An evil merry-go round,

That slowly drives you insane.

There's no turning back now,

This is my only way out.

I have a future of battle and trauma,

No doubt.

Is it worth all of this?

The troubles in my head.

I could just go back to being me,

Getting drunk instead.

I know it won't be easy,

Getting my life back on track.

But I am worth it,

I want the old me back.

Eventually the clouds part,

And I see a shaft of light.

Things start to get easier,

And my future looks bright.

Rainbows appear,

The sun starts to pour.

My feelings change,

I love myself once more.

A new life begins,

A journey of self-discovery.

Now I thank my lucky stars,

For my beautiful recovery.

The Jester and the Fool

Andreas Theologou

Part 2

Strings are pulled and chains alike,

For I dance to the tune,

That makes false emotions.

The sky has cleared,

And clarity struck,

Like the lightning of a thousand powerful strikes.

It's painful,

Or it isn't this.

I am unsure,

But what is sure is the justice,

That I should have left alone.

Hope betrayed me,

As did the clouds of the forgiven.

But never trusted nor forgotten storm,

I leave you as you left me,

In confusion and no great deal of explanation,

That only time has exposed me to.

In the right moment,

Having mercy upon me,

Like a great watcher of the souls.

Time to bid farewell to false hopes,

And untrue friends.

The battle was fierce,

But my freedom I declare from you,

No longer chained.

Happy Holidays

Deb

H appy, happy, happy.

Day four of our great holiday.

Excitedly skipping to the beach,

With our two sons.

Husband strolling behind with the bags.

He's not been the same,

Since the redundancy fourteen months ago.

A mazing, sun, sea, and sand.

We rush into the cold water,

Splashing as we go.

Screams of shock and excitement fill the air.

Husband, now on the beach,

Laughter on his face. All is fun.

P layed in the sea.

Searched in the rock pools.

Built sandcastles,

Now playing rounders.

Husband happily joins in with some fun.

Lots of laughter, lots of smiles.

Y es, I say to myself.

      I really feel that all is good.
      I smile at the boys,
      Still playing gleefully.
      Husband near me, nodding now, calm.
      Phew, it's time for me to relax a little.
      The best of days.

H usband has been great so far.

      I look up and smile, stress dissolving.
      He glances at me, then reaches for his bag,
      Tired and bleary eyed.
      Perhaps it's the busy fun of the day,
      Happily exhausted from joining in.
      He's not used to it.

O h no, my heart sinks.

      Husband pulls out a half empty bottle,
      Of pop?
      I don't think it's Irn-Bru.

L ooking forward towards me,

      With defiant eyes.
      He knows. I know.
      I lower my head and say nothing.

I watch him,

> Glug down the "pop" thirstily.
> Thankfully, boys still playing,
> Oblivious.

D aring to give a quiet sigh.

> His eyes flash anger.
> Time to leave.
> I quickly gather our things,
> And shout for the boys,
> Letting them know it's time to go.

A rriving back at the apartment,

> The boys had ran ahead.
> My husband close behind me.
> All the way home,
> He muttered vile words,
> Through sour smelling breath.
> Thankfully, the boys had gone straight to
> their rooms.
> I go in, kiss their innocent faces good night.
> But they are no longer oblivious.

Y ou always think,

> Things will get better, don't you?
> I go to our room,
> Swallowing heartbreak,
> Silently, I close the door.

S lap

> His hand hits my face.
> I fall to the floor.
> He strikes me again and again.
> When done, he walks away,
> Muttering with malice,
> 'It's all your fault'.
> I'm sore and bruised.
> Fun is over.
> Holiday is over.

Finding Me

Emma Day

Part 1

For as long as I can remember,

Even since I was a child,

I could never understand,

Why I felt so empty inside.

A huge, gaping hole,

With the need to fill.

Led me to the doctor,

My first anti-depressant pill.

Risky and reckless,

My life would soon become,

For fucks sake,

What have I done?

Why can't I stop?

Emotional, depressed, and anxious,

Someone please stop the clock.

Feeling frightened and hopeless,

Convinced I'd lost the plot.

Try these new tablets,

They'll help the pain to stop.

You'll see,

But for how long this time,

Please, tell me!

A Letter to you, Mam

J

Dear Mam,

Growing up was a happy, safe place. You put your life on hold to care for us and always be there. Once we were old enough, you went to work, which I suppose gave you some of your identity back other than being a wife and a mother. You also had friendships, which have lasted to this day so I guess you are a very good friend.

From my teenage years to now, you have put up with my chaotic lifestyle due to bad choices and alcohol addiction. You stood on the side-lines knowing I would fall but you were always there to pick me up.

You NEVER gave up hope.

My hope now is to stay sober and have a relationship with you, without the chaos in my life.

But Mam, not once until now did I or have I looked at you as a woman with feelings, emotions, wants and needs, hopes and dreams. You were just "Mam."

I know differently now and I want to apologise for never seeing you as you are; a sincere, caring person. I will treasure every moment with you because for the first time I realise you were always my best friend and I am happy, lucky, and honoured to have you as that.

My mam, my best friend.

Love,

J

xxx

The Steps to Sobriety

Annette Patton

A = Apathetic, alienated, abominable, aggressive, arbitrary.

L = Liar, lifeless, lazy, languish, laggard.

C = Calculating, callous, cantankerous, careless, carnage.

O = Obliterated, oblivious, obnoxious, overbearing, obtuse.

H = Harassing, harmful, heartbreaking, havoc, hateful.

O = Opinionated, offensive, opposing, objectifying, oppressive.

L = Lost, lame, lackadaisical, leech, lonely.

I = Impossible, ignorant, insane, intolerable, indiscreet.

C = Cynical, criminal, conniving, condescending, cruel.

S = Significant, sincere, successful, strong, spiritual.

O = Open-minded, organised, optimistic, observant, one-of-a-kind.

B = Blessed, brave, boundless, blooming, beautiful.

R = Radiant, refreshed, rejoiced, rational, resilient.

I = Idyllic, improved, insight, inspired, impartial.

E = Enthusiastic, energised, empathetic, excited, educated.

T = Triumphant, tolerant, thriving, thoughtful, thankful.

Y = Yes, yes, yes, yes, yes to SOBRIETY!

Daddy

Anonymous

I remember the day my daughter turned to me, a
serious look on her pretty, little face and said,

'Daddy, why do your eyes never smile?'

She had a concerned, furrowed brow as if the
weight of the world lay in her tiny hands.
I looked at her, mute for a moment before I let out a
silly laugh and said,

**'Don't be daft, eyes don't smile. I smile with
my mouth,'** giving her a big cheesy grin, that of
course was fake – I was sad inside despite having
such a wonderful gift of a daughter.
I knew exactly what she meant and had to pretend.

As a six year old, of course she wouldn't give up and
kept talking,

'But your eyes are so sad, Daddy, like a beasts.'

My heart suddenly felt the weight of an elephant as her innocent eyes bore into my soul.

My own Dad had the same lifeless, cold, glassy eyes of alcoholism, coloured bloodshot and yellow.

It was my moment, my wake-up call of the loudest alarm imaginable. These days, I can't say my eyes always smile but they curl up in the right direction.

The Jester and the Fool

Andreas Theologou

<u>Part 3</u>

The cut of a thousand blades,

The burning of the hottest fire,

A relief,

In contrast to me.

The endless war rages,

In my head,

Like a mad man.

A war I suspect,

Will never be won or lost.

The forefront of many battles.

The cause of this war,

Is your convincing,

And yet untrue remarks.

The fact is,

I deserve freedom.

I deserve happiness.

This I know,

But cannot be convinced.

These false hopes and tales,

Must end and soon.

I have been humiliated,

In defeat again.

But this time I strike,

Whilst my opponent rests,

After a long exhaustion,

Unsuspecting.

Finding Me

Emma Day

<u>Part 2</u>

Not long before it went wrong,

Spiraling out of control,

I'm back in that hole.

Left broken in pieces,

And torn in two,

All I want is to be happy,

Not feeling so blue.

All meds, exhausted,

I fear the worst.

Has my whole life,

Been cursed?

Talking Therapy,

Is now what you need,

But talking things through,

Made my heart bleed.

Counselling, therapy,

It went on and on.

Not getting much from it,

Do I even belong?

Maybe it's time for people,

To play my funeral song.

I am defeated,

Nothing else to give,

Can't fake being strong,

Not sure I want to live.

Better Me

Anonymous

Better me,

Evolved from the,

Trauma of painful,

Tragedy that,

Engulfed my mind and body.

Recovery gave,

Me the motivation to,

Exist.

Winter Wonderful

Deb

Happy, happy, happy.
>Excitedly, me and the boys,
>Rush down the stairs into the living room.
>Their eyes wide with excitement,
>Santa has been!
>Can hear husband coming down the stairs,
>Ho-ho-hoing!
>He's more relaxed now he's been offered a job,
>Starting after the new year.

Amazing, what a wonderful sight!
>I've pulled back the curtains,
>There's a beautiful blanket of pure snow,
>Covering the ground.
>The boys are doubly excited now,
>More fun to be had.

Presents are opened in front of the glowing fire.
>Twinkling lights are dancing on the tree,
>Cascading rainbow colours onto the wall.
>Lots of cries of joys from the boys,

Having received the gifts they'd hoped for.
Husband happy with his jumper,
Though he's forgotten to get something for
me.
I assure him it's okay.
Keep things happy.
We have breakfast then wrap up warm,
And run into the garden.
We gasp as the cold air catches our breath.
Husband stays inside for now.

Playing about,
Snowball fights,
Snowman building,
And making snow angels.
Freezing but laughing so much.
Husband did join in some.

You know, I do believe this Christmas could be
good.
We come inside, into the warmth of the
house.
Wet clothes changed,
Snuggled under blankets.
Time for hot chocolate and marshmallows.
Husband insists he will make them.

Everyone seems so happy.

Check; meats, potatoes, Brussels sprouts, carrots,
            turnip.
            All the trimmings and condiments.
            Table looks great,
            Husband had prepared it all,
            As we drank our hot chocolate.
            It had taken him a while,
            But it was lovely of him,
            I take over to cook.
            All in our seats, dinner served and eaten.
            Boys have left their sprouts!
            Husband pops a bottle of fizz, grinning.
            One glass for a toast,
            Merry Christmas, all is good.

Hoping family will drop by to say hello.
            They were here last year, It was a great day.
            I knew lunch today was off the menu for
            them.
            Haven't seen Mam and Dad since the
            holiday.
            The boys and I stayed with them for a few
            days.
            We do talk on the phone though,

Brother and sister included.
To let them know I'm okay.

Ready for family games now, more fun.
Husband plays with the boys on their new PS games.
They are laughing and teasing one another,
Each one is desperate to win!
My turn to play, we choose Twister.
Husband vetoes this, offers to do the dishes.
How kind.
Hand red, foot blue, hand yellow, foot green.
Lots of laughter as we bend and fall.

It feels like today has been the happiest for a while.
That's the magic of Christmas.
I've always loved this time of year.
Photos have been taken at every chance,
Building fond memories,
To look back on and remember.

So sad, family didn't visit.
They did ring though.
Boys thanked them for their presents,
And excitedly told them all about their day.

Hoped they would see them soon.
I took the phone, said I understood,
They couldn't visit and it was lovely to hear
their voices.
Mam and I laughed,
A few tears too.
Hoped we would meet up soon,
And I love them.

This has still been a really lovely day.
I look around the room,
The sparkling decorations,
The tree with its dancing lights,
And the scattered presents.
Boys are back on their game.
Husband looks bleary eyed but offers to
make cups of tea.
He's probably tired from the busy day.
He hands me the tea,
My eyes dart to his other hand,
Wrapped around a large glass of Irn-Bru.
A familiar flash in his eyes.
Head lowered, say nothing.

My heart sinks.
I drink half of my tea then get up,

I head to the kitchen.
Don't look at him.
I open the tea towel drawer,
Underneath is a nearly empty bottle,
Of Irn-Bru, though I know it's not.
It's all so clear now – his help, his kindness.
I steady myself and walk into the living room.
'Come on, boys,' I say cheerfully,
'Time for showers.'
Boys look at me, curiously questioning.
Then they look at their dad,
Before heading upstairs.
I sit on the dining room chair,
He knows I know.

Again I dared to hope.
        As you have to have hope,
        Don't you?
        Husband walks towards me,
        Where I sit, deflated,
        Empty glass on the shelf.

Slams his fist,
        Bang the table,
        Again and again.
        Leaning towards me as he spits,

Vileness from his sour, smelling breath.
I look away,
It's not him,
It's the demon inside him.
He steps away, muttering.
I make him act like this.
No soreness or bruising this time.
I go to kiss the boys good night.
Christmas is over,
Fun is over.

Moving Forward

Annette Patton

Stuck in a whirlpool of addiction,

It's not meant for me.

Is a residential detox,

Where I really want to be?

I've tried reducing my alcohol,

On my own,

But I always find another full bottle,

Lying around my home.

Those hidden bottles,

That I'd forgotten about,

When left with nothing,

I would seek them out.

Sat drinking from hour to hour,

I really have got no willpower.

Residential detox is what I really need,

Or in four or five months, I'll be deed.

Travelling to Manchester for my detox,

My head's all over,

My stomach, a big knot.

My body is aching, shaking,

Feeling red hot.

A week of hell is what I fear,

From other people's rehab, that I hear.

Then we arrive, it isn't a dive,

But still I wondered if I'll make it out alive.

Day One - cold turkey wasn't the word,

'It's medication time, Annette,'

Was all I heard.

Along came the doctor with a needle and pen,

Jabbed me in the arse, told me to 'Count to 10.'

Day Two - the shakes, sweats, itchiness,

The unwanted thoughts set in.

I knew before getting better,

It would first become more grim.

Especially as they came back,

To jab another needle in!

Day Three - I ached from head to toe,

My arse bruised, tender and sore.

If the nurse was throwing a javelin,

She'd get a 10/10 score!

Not wanting to move,

Or give any activities a go.

I just laid on the bed,

Praying my confidence would grow.

Feeling worse than ever before,

I felt sick and numb to the core.

Day Four - I woke up feeling a little different.

My mood had lifted,

Not feeling such an irritant.

Is this the break through I'd been longing for?

My meds reduced and my arse not as sore.

Day Five - I actually feel alive,

You know what?

I think after all,

I'm going to survive.

Day Six - I'm starting to feel great,

I'm looking forward,

Without the hate.

Starting to believe I could be okay,

If I keep going this way.

Day Seven – A little flame burns in me,

Of the future ahead,

The way it could be.

I've hope, I can do it,

Support is there.

People care about me,

And now I also care.

<u>Everywhere</u>

Paul

When I was younger, I didn't know,

That alcohol could make you so low.

The advice wasn't there,

For me to take care,

And avoid the addiction that was coming my way.

The adverts are everywhere,

And the alcohol is there for you,

To buy without a care.

In everyday life, it's in your face,

On TV in adverts,

And when you fill up at the petrol garage.

It's hard to avoid when it's in the shops,

With walls of alcohol for you,

To walk past when you go into shop.

When I go to buy a stamp,

It's in the post office too.

How do you avoid it looking at you?

The temptation is there,

So you have to take care,

To avoid the alcohol acting like a snare.

When I was young if only I was told,

What harm could be done,

It could have made a difference,

To what I had become.

Finding Me

Emma Day

Part 3

Then an answer appeared,
For me to be in control,
Self-medicating filled,
That painful, empty hole.
I thought that drink and drugs,
Weren't for mugs.
They made me feel confident,
Untouchable, and free,
The bottle and bag,
Became my best friend, you see.
But this certainly wasn't reality.
Guilt and shame,
Began to swallow me whole,
NO POSITIVES,
No end goal.
Screaming and kicking inside,
I wanted to isolate,
I wanted to hide.

Claire's Story

Claire Lindoe

As a child growing up, I lived with my nana. This was because my dad was in the Army and I also had three siblings. My mam couldn't cope so Nana helped out. I settled in a school and made friends but every time this happened, I was picked back up by my mam and my dad and taken back to live with them. This repeated for my full childhood.

My life was never settled, disrupted wherever I was living. I never had a friend for long, uprooted constantly. This carried on throughout my life up until now but my nana was always my strength and guidance.

I partied with friends as a I grew up but also went on outings with my family. I remember always laughing, crying at times but I was never angry. I got on with life, the good and bad. Then my world fell apart – I lost my nana.

I felt alone, my life turned for the worst. It all came in on me and began to crumble. I had been a hard worker and a loving wife but the loss of Nana impacted heavily. Then lock down came and my old friends dwindled away. The same happened with my family as we were all forced apart and there was a void of Nana in my world.

My new best friend was cocaine. This was the greatest friend you could imagine at the beginning. Amazing and never let me down until it became the devil and then turned me into the devil. I started being violent to the only person I had in my life, my wife. My violence, the lying and bad behaviours became who I was.

I wasn't myself I was what cocaine had made me. My world was deteriorating. Everything around me was being destroyed.

I was employed in a well-paid job and a role I was happy in. The devil I had become resulted in me calling in sick, not bothered about consequence –

treating myself and others badly. I had lost my control, powerless. The devil controlled me. I was no longer Claire, I had become someone no one recognised.

Cocaine had made me a monster.

I was a total mess and this lasted around two and a half years. I hit my lowest point and put my foot down, telling the devil it was time to go – Claire had to take control back and come out strong.

I searched and searched for the help I needed and I found Recovery Connections. I believe this changed my life and helped me get my life back, making me even stronger than before the devil took over. I have now completed 12 steps of recovery. It's not been easy but I have put 100% into changing my bad behaviours.

I am proud to say I am currently five months clean from the devil and my life has changed massively.

I am so much more positive, see a future and have many plans to give recovery back to anyone who needs it in the future.

I am now Claire and I am not the devil.

Dedicated to my nana.

The Jester and the Fool

Andreas Theologou

Part 4

The Jester,

The Fool,

The names I have carried,

And been known by.

I bring humour,

Sadness,

Loyalty.

I bring excitement on my back,

But laughed at I am.

Awoken from dream tales,

And pain,

From which I have seen,

And lived,

Shall be wiped through clean,

Like a thief of a king.

No more a jester,

Or a fool.

For those whose care meet no needs,

I seek vengeance,

For the pain.

Yet beyond a fool,

I see nobody is to blame,

But me.

Causation is futile,

When the ribbon holding,

Falls like a leaf from a tree.

Darkness or light,

Are two options available to me.

Grey comes and visits,

To remind of a life,

Unworthy to me.

The jester is free,

But the fool

remains.

The chains he

breaks to the grey,

Are never seen.

<u>Colour</u>

J

It was a dark, autumn morning. I walked into the room, shaking and angry at the thought of not having that drink.

What was the point in this?
No one could help me out of this miserable, dark, black and white life I had led for the past 30 years.

As the weeks went by, you encouraged me, supported me, and gave me knowledge of what seemed to be some kind of life outside of this pain.

I started to see the colours of the autumn leaves falling from the balding trees.
I became aware of my surroundings. You gave me strength, to carry on with this journey.

There was hope.

You introduced me to Recovery Connections.

Amazed, inspired and in awe of the positivity within this community.

Like the branches of the balding trees, reaching to the sky, I ventured more and more out of my comfort zone.

I began to see more colour and during a trip out to Farne Islands, I found **my whole body engulfed in peace, harmony, and tranquility**.

The spiritual awareness of freedom was real.
Now I knew the feeling of those branches, now in full bloom, reaching to the sky. Standing tall and strong in their beauty.

My life is no longer dark, no longer in black and white.

My life is full of colour, happiness, and laughter.
I will always be eternally grateful to **Recovery Connections** and hold the community dear in my heart.

Dedicated to Wendy Redman, CGL, Houghton-le-Spring

Dear Alcohol

Annette Patton

When I was all alone,

You crept in,

made me drop my phone.

Cleverly crawled in,

Worked your way into my zone.

We sat and kissed goodbye,

To ever being alone.

Those dark days and endless nights,

Seemed to pass so quick.

But you kept shouting,

'C'mon Annette, have another sip.'

As I took another drink,

You made my problems disappear.

Until those demons in my head,

Was all I could hear.

I was fighting hard,

To give up the drink,

To keep my friends and family near.

Then there you were, yet again,

'C'mon Annette, have another beer.'

No escaping you,

A pain in my heart,

A pain in my rear.

A residential detox,

Seemed the only way to go,

To make life happy,

Dissolve the low.

Alcohol, you put me through hell.

But I'm here,

I've got a story to live,

And to tell.

Finding Me

Emma Day

Part 4

Come on girl,

You've got this,

STAY STRONG!

You've been here before,

You must soldier on.

Yes, you do belong,

STAY POSITIVE, KEEP FIGHTING ON.

Meeting new people,

Inspiring, incredibly strong.

Knowing I'm not the only one,

Who thought they didn't belong.

Oh God,

I've looked at life so wrong.

It wasn't my fault,

I WASN'T TO BLAME.

Stop with the guilt,

Embarrassment and shame.

WE ARE RECOVERY CONNECTIONS,

Let us help you win this game.

We are here beside you,

You've so much to gain.

We're your friends,

We're your family,

Let us walk you through the rain.

With their help and support,

I finally understood.

That my life could be bright,

Bold and good.

Easter Eggcellence

Deb

Happy, happy, happy.
Excitedly with my two boys,
I run into the garden for egg hunt!
Husband is already there.
He's been hiding the eggs in the most
difficult places possible.
Boys are so excited,
They're getting older – who knows if this fun
will happen next year.
Husband has a big grin on his face.
The days have been much happier,
Since he started work just over three months
ago.

Amazing!
I look around as the crispness of spring
caresses our faces.
The trees are blossoming,
The plants are sprouting,
The daffodils are in full bloom.
The sun is trying to break through the clouds.
New life, fresh beginnings.
All is good.

Pushing and shoving,
> The boys compete to find the most eggs.
> They have equal amounts, one left,
> Husband nods to me in the direction of the
> last egg.
> Boys spot him.
> I run and they try to take me down.
> I'm quicker, I grab the egg.
> No winner to boast, ha!
> Lots of laughter, lots of fun.
> Such a lovely morning.
> We're thirsty so have a drink and a rest.

Parents are here for lunch.
> I'm so excited to see them.
> They hug and kiss the boys,
> Then apprehensively, Dad shakes husband's
> hand,
> And Mam pecks his cheek.
> We sit down for a cuppa and a chat.
> Husband makes the tea, the boys drink pop.
> Tears of laughter fall from our faces,
> As the boys re-enact the Easter hunt.
> I look at husband, he appears relaxed.
> I smile – all is going lovely.

Yes! We've decided to play another game.
     Guess the animal – rabbit, mouse, snake,
     kangaroo.
     We yell at one another, wanting to be right.
     Mam wins with a monkey impersonation.
     Now that was funny!
     Our cheeks ache with laughter,
     Time for lunch.

Everything is set out. Check;
     Lamb, roast potatoes, carrots, turnip,
     cauliflower, Yorkshire puds and condiments.
     Husband and I worked together,
     Though at times, he took a break.
     We all sit down, we have a toast,
     With Nosecco – cheers to happiness.
     Husband grimaces.
     Lots of chatter as we eat.
     I look around at the faces,
     All look relaxed and happy.

Absolutely confident this is going to be the best day
     in a long time.
     Dinner is finished, dessert to go.
     Husband insists he serves, how kind.

He disappears into the kitchen, gone a little while.
Family look apprehensively,
I try to smile, reassuringly.
Dessert is served to parents first, manners important.
Then back for ours.
Appearing from the kitchen, he stumbles a little.
Husband laughs, family gasp.
I muster a smile.

So lunch is over, out comes the camera.
Family photos snapped,
First time in a while, everyone together.
Laughter, fun, face pulling, and animal acting.
A lovely photo of husband, me, and the boys.
All smiling.
So happy.

The family have left.
Husband in the room, playing with the boys.
Today has been heaven.
I look into the room, boys are on their games,

Competing as usual!
Husband looks tired, heavy eyed.
He glances at me. I smile, lower my head,
And go into the kitchen.
Most of it is tidy, husband has helped a lot.
So kind, so lovely.
I put the dishes away – cutlery, then the
glasses.
I open the pan cupboard, I pause.
My heart races for seconds,
I see the half bottle of Irn-Bru.
I close the door.
The boys had that today – no sinking
feelings, no fear.

Everything these days is calm,
Busy still though.
Husband has his job and is happy with it.
We try to work as a team.
We still have words, now and then,
But that's normal.
Boys are calm,
School grades are up.
I couldn't be happier at this moment.

Recovery for addiction,
Counsellors for mental health and group sessions,
Have been a great support for us over the last few months.
Husband's determination to be his true self,
Was his choice to make.
Happily, he did.
I've always said you have to have hope,
Don't you?
We will crack this with all the support we have,
And move forward,
As a happy family, well most of the time.

All is good.

The Jester and the Fool

Andreas Theologou

Part 5

I am sorry,

For not leaving.

Hope betrayed.

And now I see clear,

Your care a manifestation,

Of my lonely imagination.

I should have left,

Not entering your life,

At a different scene.

It's now I realise,

I'm a fool,

And I am sorry,

For not leaving things,

As they were.

In peace,

Sadness will not fall upon you.

For the jester matters,

Not to you.

I declare my exit.

With a spell,

I shall be wiped clean,

From your memory.

Tried but divided,

I am love,

Or hate,

I am unsure.

Fear of the revelation,

Too big to comprehend.

I am sorry,

I should have left you,

In peace.

Love or hate,

The attempt was made,

But failed.

I demand too much,

You give little or less.

Time the ribbons are cut,

For the jester,

To be free,

The war is won.

I skip to freedom,

Towards what my heart desires.

Time has revealed what is right.

I should have allowed peace,

Fool.

Dear Crack

Joanne

It's been a while,

Since I last had a pipe with you.

And to be honest,

I don't miss you.

I never thought I would say that.

I'm happy I've said goodbye,

To the endless, sleepless nights,

Not forgetting the hours I wasted,

In the rain,

Waiting for you to be dropped off.

And I'm really glad to say,

Hopefully,

I will never do that again.

From,

Joanne

Finding Me

Emma Day

Part 5

My mental health,

I misunderstood:

PTSD, it's my traumas that broke me,

ADHD and BPD were the problems, you see,

And I let them consume me.

Understanding my illnesses and how to cope,

Give me an insight, provided hope.

In RECOVERY now and battling on,

Teaching myself how to be strong.

With people like myself,

Who also know they belong.

Good days and bad days,

There will always be.

But I won't let the bad days,

Capture me.

My LIFE now SO PRECIOUS to me,

Husband,

Kids,

Friends and family.

I love them so much,

 I can't comprehend,

Not being with them,

Until the very end.

My story, I've told,

My story will continue,

As I tell myself:

'Emma, you now have the strength within YOU.'

Me and my beautiful family

Dedicated to my amazing family and friends

My loving family, without all of your support, I wouldn't be where I am today. I love you all so very much. Love always from your wife, your mam, your daughter, your cousin, and your best friend, Emma. xxx

Dear my Best Friend, C@*t!
(AKA alcohol)

Anonymous

You've helped me when I've been anxious, needing comfort. When I've been sad, you've been there.

You've gave me the courage when I've lacked confidence and brought me fun times, bursts of happiness. But mostly you've gave me excruciating pain and sadness as you became an enemy.

You've made me feel worthless, like a piece of shit and that the world would be a better place without me. That I was nothing but an oxygen thief and that perhaps I should just kill myself.

Would I even be missed? Real friends build you up and bring out the best in each other, but not you.

Not you alcohol. You fucking horrible c@*t!

I don't need you anymore. You're not my friend.

Free

Laurie Crow

They asked me what freedom feels like,

I liken it to a song.

The one from Gladiator,

'Now We Are Free,'

Hans Zimmer, couldn't get it wrong.

What does freedom feel like?

I liken it to a day,

Where I could have my kids alone, just me,

No social worker,

Watching us play.

What does freedom feel like?

I liken it to a calm night.

Where I drift off with gratitude,

And wake feeling I'm alive.

What does freedom feel like?

I liken it to the sky.

Where I get to look up at the stars,

This shift no longer passes me by.

Freedom feels like living,

Not surviving every day.

A life where I get to choose,

The one I choose today.

Geordie Serenity Prayer

Annette Patton

God, grant wor ta serenity,

Tuh accept ta things,

Ah canna change.

Courage tuh change,

Ta things ah can,

An wisdom tuh knar ta difference.

Livin yen da at a time,

Enjoyin yen moment at a time,

Acceptin hardship,

As tha pathwa tuh peace.

Takin, as he did,

This sinful warld,

As it is,

Not as ah wud hev it.

Trustin that he,

Will myek aaal things reet,

If ah surrenda tuh eez will.

That ah ma be reasonably happy,

In this life,

An supremely happy wi' him,

Forivvor in ta next.

Amen.

Adapted from the The Serenity Prayer attributed to Reinhold
Neibuhr)

The Jester and the Fool

Andreas Theologou

<u>Part 6</u>

In many different directions,

The light guides us.

Upon first meeting our betrayer,

The light is there,

Even if dim.

The light guides as it wills,

Goodbye betrayer.

Live your life,

Be free betrayer.

Just one last favour,

I ask of you.

Remember me dead,

As I try to keep shining,

You fool.

__My Moment__

Anonymous

Many moments led me to drink, another wine, followed by another and another until I had lost count. Lost my confidence. Lost myself.

Then I lost you and it still wasn't enough to stop. I had no reason to stop until I lost her. It was too late, she was never coming back. Gone forever like the last wine I poured down the drain, claiming I wouldn't do it again and instead I would seek help. And I did.

Her dying saved my life and now I will live for us both.

I Am a Force

Lisa Peacock

You thought you had me there,

That I'd be forever under your spell,

And I almost fell for it,

Until you made me feel unwell.

I felt like I was drowning,

My head bobbing under the water,

And I fell for your charms,

Like a lamb to the slaughter.

You tried to take me down,

But couldn't keep me there for long.

Because I'm worth fighting for.

I'm a warrior and I'm strong.

See, I'm a force to be reckoned with.

I'm stronger than I thought,

I've built myself some armour now,

The kind that can't be bought.

So back away from me,

I'm the only winner here.

I'm bigger than you,

And I no longer live in fear.

Life is Beautiful

Adam Bell

In the madness of addiction,

I'd lost my way,

Fighting a losing battle,

Every single day.

The hurt I felt,

The pain I caused,

Killed me inside,

Til I felt no more.

Screaming and shouting,

Wanting to break free.

But there's that voice again,

Telling me you're not ready.

You can't do this,

You fail all the time.

You'll never be nothing,

So why even try.

You know you want me,

Pick up the phone.

He'll only be half an hour,

And the pain will be no more.

That lovely brown powder,

Cooking on the spoon.

You can taste me already,

You'll be flying to the moon.

That warm, fuzzy feeling,

That makes you feel safe.

You know you want it,

Why hesitate.

Pick up the phone,

Do it already.

You know damn well,

You'll never be nothing.

I've had enough,

I'm on my knees.

If there's a God,

HELP me,

Please!

I'm ready to surrender,

I'll give it my all.

I'm sick of all the pain,

And sadness I've caused.

I'm hurting my family,

I'm seeing them cry.

The pain and fear,

Weeping from their eyes.

Adam,

You can do this,

PLEASE,

Just one more try.

I believe in you,

I'll be there,

Right by your side.

Let's get help,

We'll do it together.

Whatever it takes,

To see you get better.

I'm doing it Mam,

I made a promise to Dad.

I'll make you proud one day,

I'll leave it at that.

Just give me the time,

I need,

To do this on my own.

I won't let you down,

Please,

Don't give up hope.

Two and a half years sober,

I've found my way.

I love the man,

I am today.

Full of gratitude,

Bursting with

pride.

I can't believe,

I made it out,

ALIVE.

I'm on a journey,

With sunshine,

On my face.

Filled with laughter,

Every single day.

Feeling happiness,

Sadness no more.

Everyday a miracle,

Walking out the door.

Finally through the battles,

I struggled and fought.

Now I'm helping others,

Giving them support.

Me, now enjoying life

Through their daily struggles,

They will succeed.

Recovery Connections,

We are family.

I made a plan, set some goals.

Within time became,

A recovery coach.

If I can do it, So can you.

My life is beautiful,

And I wish it for you.

My dogs: Gypsey, King, and Star

Dedicated to my family – for supporting me through everything and never giving up on me. Thank you. xxx

Me by the Sea

Paul

This is me,

Down by the sea,

Thinking about alcohol,

Red wine and me.

It's to the sea,

I must come to think,

What I have done.

I've been drinking,

Too long,

And something's got to be done.

So to Lifeline I go,

To let alcohol go,

It won't be easy, I know.

Going to SMART,

It will help,

I know that myself.

So it's on the recovery road, I go.

I know it may be slow,

But I will give it a go.

I'll get there,

In the end,

Without alcohol as a friend.

And my alcohol addiction,

Will end.

Then I can go,

Down by the sea.

And I will be free.

Not thinking of alcohol,

Red wine and me.

It will be just me,

By the sea.

Puddles

Anonymous

I looked in puddles for so long that my reflection

almost evaporated.

Faceless,

Feeling less,

Numb.

Until my water started flowing in a different

direction, towards a place of

Beauty,

Safety,

Calmness.

Now my reflection looks back at me, and it smiles.

The Jester and the Fool

Andreas Theologou

Part 7 – New Beginnings

As the jester roams free,

The reality is clear to the fool,

Whose chains are still intact,

Against the place the jester looks from,

The hole to his freedom.

The fool in his chains,

Behind the curtain of despair.

Hope shattered a million times.

No end of pain in sight.

The fool acknowledged his time was nigh,

Spending the rest of his days in pain.

The jester, ever optimistic,

Seeing light in the false dawns,

Where curtains where drawn all along.

After so long left in sorrow and despair,

A beaming, gleaming ray of light,

Shining through the air.

The ray of light is you.

The shattered pieces of me,

Come to life.

To give a feeling unfamiliar,

Sunlight kissing skin.

The ever beautiful touch of light,

Of hope and love.

A strange and turbulent feeling,

The fool and the jester,

Questioning what trick is at hand,

From the cruel mistress of life.

Light shining through the chains,

Freeing the fool.

Both finally free,

To feel the love and care,

That isn't a trick.

Here is to you my love,

My saviour,

My hope.

You set me free.

The Fool, The Jester.

Trying to Conquer you

Anonymous

Tempted,
Teasing,
Touched,
Tasted.
Taken,
Into a terrifying trap.
Knowing it will lead to,
Trouble,
Torment,
Trauma,
Trying to conquer you.

Living in the Madness

Emma Day

I lived in the madness - physical abuse, mental abuse, emotional abuse, sexual abuse. Grief, from losing close friends to suicide. Grief from losing close family members, gone. Experiencing several miscarriages. Myself, born with a disability that has affected my whole life. Suffering from mental ill health but for my little boy, to be born sleeping – I just couldn't cope.

My journey with addiction, where do I start?

From that first sip of cider to endless bottles of wine. Living in the madness. Day after day, turning to years. Moving on to drugs, swallowing as many ecstasy pills as I could possibly take. Snorting whizz out of a huge bag for breakfast, dinner, and tea.

A feast of narcotics.

Next step, coke,

Snorted through banknotes.

Always needing to toke,

Have a good smoke – my life became a fucking joke.

Pre-gabs and opioids,

Now I've given up hope.

Bedridden and two back surgeries to look forward to.

Fuck knows how I plodded through.

Always living life to the extreme,

Reckless,

Risky behaviour.

Afraid of no danger.

Then finally a diagnosis for my mental health; borderline personality disorder, post-traumatic stress disorder, ADHD with a splash of alcohol and drug misuse disorder. Things start to become more clear to me as I trudge through the darkness,

through the desperation to try and gain my life back.

Wanting the anger inside to stop, not wanting
to feel empty, lost, with a desire to no longer exist.
Suicide often feels like a gift. I don't want to go, to
isolate myself. But I'm riddled with guilt, shame
consuming me like a shark swallowing its prey.

I've failed as a mother,

A wife,

A daughter and a friend.

Someday,

I will make amends.

Fear of abandonment,

Cuts my soul deep.

All I do, is sit and weep.

Me and my dad

Lonely and heartbroken, existing in the madness. Someone, please help me find a sense of purpose. I need to be back in the real world, all I want is another chance at life.

Addiction,

Fuck you!

You stole my life.

The clarity forming,

This is no kind of life.

Me and my mam

It's time for me,

To be free.

The journey I've travelled,

Enduring much pain.

I realise now,

I've so much to gain.

Addiction,

You won't win this game!

Me and Lois

Recovery Connections,

This was my aim.

Feeling positive,

Hopeful, and strong.

You gave me the courage,

To battle on.

And now, with confidence,

I know I belong.

With acceptance and courage,

Fearless, I will be.

Me and Sarah

Recovery,

Is a gift to me.

Back in the real world,

This is now me.

Connecting with others,

Friends and family.

Recovery Connections,

You set me free.

I'm living life with gratitude.

Feeling humble,

A positive attitude.

Always striving for better things,

Recovery Connections,

This is what it brings.

Empathy,

Understanding,

Healing,

Support.

So special to me,

They gave me my wings,

Now I can fly free.

Me and Adam

Recovery Connections were there and as I took each step, they remained by my side. Always supporting, always encouraging. The most portant

thing in life for me is being here, in this moment. I'm with my beautiful family, my world.

A mother and a wife,

A daughter,

And a friend.

The life I now cherish,

Until the very end.

Me and my husband, Ali

Dedicated to my children – Nathan, Kane, Darcie, and my angel son, Ellis. Also for my husband, Ali, my mam and dad, my whole family, and amazing friends.

Poison

Anonymous

An addictive poison that's toxic to my life, my mind,

my body.

Toxic to my relationship, family, career.

Poison that needs to be cut out,

Removed,

Drained.

So I can heal, repair, and renew.

Alcohol, my poison, it's you.

The Gift

Thomas Dale

Not a flash car or a fancy home.

I give you recovery.

It is a seed encased in moist earth.

It promises hope,

Like the delicate flutter of a butterfly.

Here.

Its path will have you,

On the verge of despair,

Like a forsaken beacon,

On a turbulent night.

It will make you crave,

The erroneous security of your vice,

Solace in the intimate alliance once forged.

I am only being honest.

Not a false dream or fool's gold.

I give you recovery.

Its flickering flame will guide your way,

Blazing and bright

As a phoenix,

Rerisen from the smouldering ash.

Take it.

It's a gift that cannot be given,

At most, inspired.

Yours now.

A burden to carry,

I truthfully know.

It'll lighten, I'm sure,

As you strengthen and grow.

Like the stubborn clutches,

Of darkness,

With the ensuing dawn.

Infectious.

Its change will guide others,

Lead them to life.

Relapse

Laurie Crow

I thought that I was doing great,

I'd managed to get a grip.

The ups they kept on coming,

I was never going to stop.

I forgot for a little while,

That my mind is a haven.

For thoughts that creep,

At the strangest times,

And remind me that I'm human.

No one has it all worked out,

Not even those who are sound.

So why did I think I was different,

That I'd never hit the ground.

It's a journey, not a destination,

I hear it all the time.

Allow myself the space to breathe,

And for not always getting it right.

The thought of using comes to me,

At strange times, day and night.

When I'm mad, when I'm strong,

Even more when things are going right.

The journey means to keep on going,

The bad times we know will lift.

And maybe then I can realise,

That the bad times – they were a gift.

Shining

Andy Neville

I never thought I'd be where I am today.

Crack came into my life some 18 months ago and seemed harmless when I first started using it. However, let me tell you, it slowly started changing me from an honest, hard-working man to a liar. I was soon closed off, a subdued drug user who would either be using or if not, thinking about using. It consumed me.

Crack took my driving licence from me along with £25,000! It stole my true happiness and more.

Hear me when I tell you that I'm fighting back. I'm owning my addiction. I began being honest with myself and people I needed to tell – my parents, my son's mum.

I started my recovery journey and I'm still on it. I know I need more help, that's why I'm going into rehab, to get free. Free from the hold of that nasty stuff called crack.

I was created to shine not to be isolated and a fraction of the real me.

Crack, you're not my friend.

My Addiction

Vicky Lowery

My addiction to alcohol,

Has left me broken.

I've had many bruises,

Many scars.

I have fought,

Every step,

Of my journey.

I have survived,

My addiction,

Battling to the end.

My life now back, mine,

And looking to the future,

With my son.

Thanks to **Gateshead Recovery Connections** with day rehab – you saved my life.

__Sleep__

Scott Knights

My cry,

Into the night.

A battle,

I moan into sleep.

The whirling laughter,

Of my demons.

The gloom,

The darkness,

Of my sleep.

I wake,

Shaking in triumph.

Bright thoughts,

Shooting from,

All corners,

Of my mind.

Today,

I have victory.

Tomorrows, far behind.

A Work in Progress

Anonymous

It wasn't always bad,

Else it would never have felt good.

But for the snippets of high,

The lows overflowed.

Like the bad memories into puddles on the ground.

That never dried out in the hottest sun,

Instead, had to be healed from within.

My mind a broken glass,

That was delicately repaired.

Cracks still there,

Still fragile,

But whole.

My Story

Ann D

At around the age of six years old, I was sexually abused continuously until the age of 15. My abuser was my biological father, but I can't bring myself to ever think of him as a father, merely the person who supplied the sperm to my mother's egg. I watched him beat my mother and older brother for years. He threatened me that if I ever told anyone he would hurt me and my mother in a really bad way. I was so scared, I never said a word to anyone.

I was 15 years old when I found out he was also abusing my cousin and two of my friends. He made me feel so guilty, how did I not realise he was abusing them as well as me? If only I had spoken up when my own abuse started perhaps he would have never touched them.

Things finally came to a head in 1984 when I was 15 years old. At last, I somehow found the courage and told all to my mother. She promptly took me to the police station, where I gave a statement and subsequently, he was arrested and jailed for a mere three years! I felt that it was not enough and justice has not been served. On release, having only served one year with good behaviour, he was tagged. Members of the public verbally abused him, having heard the stories about him. But I have also suffered the injustice of being shouted at in the street. To this day, nearly 40 years later, I still hear whispers and snide comments directed towards me.

I was 18 years old when I first had my son. I brought him up by myself before going on to have a further four sons and one daughter. I was in an extremely bad relationship; violence and abuse were the norm. The result was that I had three of my sons taken into care, in 1987.

I moved to Houghton but later returned to Sunderland where I struggled to get help from local services. In 1989, I was admitted to Cherry Knowles Hospital with a severe mental breakdown – life had become too much and I simply couldn't cope.

After leaving the hospital, I tried to rebuild my life, having a son in a new relationship. The man wanted us to move to Newcastle and once again, violence entered the relationship to the extent that social services intervened and my son was taken away from me. I didn't stand a chance. I left the relationship and in 1991, I met my first husband. We had two sons, but once again, destiny took a hand and this didn't work out. We divorced with joint custody, although our children lived with me.

I remarried in 2001 and have now been married for 21 years. However, trauma continued to follow me and I discovered that my daughter was abused by my stepson. My nightmare was back again and I didn't know how much more I could take. My stepson was arrested and sentenced to six years in prison.

In 2013, social services came to my door to inform me that my biological father had cancer and all I thought was, *what do you want me to do*? He had put me down as his next of kin. I reluctantly went to the hospital to visit and all I saw was a frail old man, not the big, butch bastard that beat up my mother and abused me. I swallowed my pride and went towards him. He asked for my forgiveness, but I told him

'NO, NEVER.'

He left all his insurance to me. I never shed a tear, instead, I claimed the insurance money and took my daughter to Benidorm for her 16th birthday.

In 2014, my other stepson passed away. I was so close to him and was truly heartbroken. Then in 2019, loss presented itself again after my precious mother passed away in front of me, at my house. Her last words were,

'I love you.'

My whole world fell apart, had I not been through enough for one person in their lifetime? I could no longer cope at all and took the obvious escape route, turning to drink, finally becoming dependent on it, desperate to numb the pain of a lifetime.

Alcohol became my medicine but it never made things better for long, instead, it began to kill me and the remaining people in my life that I cared about had to witness it.

Eventually, I discovered WEAR Recovery, Recovery Connections and other support groups. They welcomed me and made me feel supported and worthy. I have since been diagnosed with bipolar, PTSD and psychosis, but with the help of the correct medication, I am holding up well enough. All the support around me helps massively.

I'm nine months sober now and looking forward to my future, instead of dying from drinking. I have holidays, taking in all the sights, the beautiful sand, the blue sea, the sunshine and lying back sunbathing. I can now go on holiday, not spending money on a substance that would kill me. I'm determined to see more sites of the world and explore. Only now, I will be sober and really take things in so that I can have beautiful memories. My coping strategy is singing and I love hitting the karaoke, thinking of Mam as I blast out a few songs, remembering the good times singing songs from musicals on a Sunday afternoon.

I would like to say thank you to my facilitator at recovery connections, Wendy, for the inspiration and to all the people in the group for their strength and support. Remember, if I can do it, anyone can with the right help and support. When that devil raises his head just say NO and have a cuppa and chat with people who understand.

I hope you all do well. if you are reading this story then just take a step back people, you're not alone, there is always light at the end of the tunnel.

Ann D

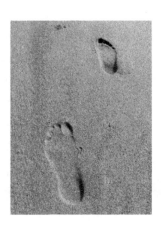

The Devil's Piss Water

Paul

Supermarkets.

Walking along the supermarket isles,

Past all the beer and wine.

It makes you want to drink.

Think of it as the devil's piss water,

And it will make you want to vomit.

Then you can walk past it,

And not be tempted to drink.

It will get you through another week,

Until you go shopping again.

The devil's piss water will always be there,

So avoid it at all costs.

Or it will cost you dearly,

(Think of the cost to you so far).

If you are tempted to take a drink,

It really does taste awful,

If you think of it like that.

The devil will always be tempting you,

To make you want to drink.

So don't be tempted to drink his piss,

Or the devil,

He will win.

Dear Love

Jacqueline Jordan

Dear Love,

I'd known you all my life, always a part of my family. I didn't notice when I started falling for you. In the beginning you were amazing. You gave me a voice, gave me the confidence I'd craved my whole life. You made me believe in myself and told me that yes, I could sing that song beautifully.

I loved you so much that I didn't notice when the relationship I had with you began to slowly, slowly turn abusive. I didn't notice when **you started controlling me**, when you started to stop me from seeing my friends and eventually my family. I made excuses when you knocked me out and I blamed myself when I couldn't face that appointment I had because I couldn't face leaving you.

I still believed I was a good mum because you didn't stop me from loving them, going to work, or keeping my house clean. What I didn't realise was that my babies were seeing you abuse me and they **felt helpless**. They felt that they had to look after me. You made my babies into little adults. I can never forgive you for that, never. But I still needed you. How messed up is that?

You messed up my whole world. My family fell apart. You controlled me and yet I still desperately needed you. I attempted to leave you so many times but when I tried, you tortured me. I was alone in my house and you still tricked me into seeing and hearing things which weren't there. You made me sweat and shake. I always came back to you because then the torture would stop. You made me ill, taking my family from me and making people who once loved me despise me.

I've got something to let you know though, a secret I've been keeping from you.

Haha, I've been cheating on you! I've been seeing lots of **people who are slowly helping me**. I haven't left you yet, but I will. They are making me **feel strong again**. They are showing me what my future could be without you. I love each and every one of them because they love me. Not like you who just wants to control me.

This is my letter to you, alcohol. I will leave you soon and will never let your poison or your controlling ways enter my body again.

So I lift my glass of water or Pepsi Max to give a toast to being free again.

Lots of hate,
Jacqueline

Dedicated to my recovery family – James, Java Pen, Hannah, Mum and Dad, without any of you, I wouldn't be here now. Love you all.

My Sobriety

Annette Patton

I've kept going, working on that rollercoaster ride I call "SOBRIETY."

I decided to drink that last glass of wine (24/05/22) and travel down the challenging and very rocky road to recovery. It's not been plain sailing. Some good days and some horrendous days but I can honestly say

my

    horrendous

        days

            sober

                are

                    100%

                        better

                      than

                my

           best

      days

drunk.

I think more clearly now. I remember things. I can make better decisions and I'm 100% more rational! All of these things that evil alcohol stole from me.

My anxiety and depression are slowly but surely slipping away. I'm able to comfortably interact and have connections with others. I volunteer with **Recovery Connections** and enrolled on an ambassadors course.

If I can give someone a little glimmer of hope like what was given to me I'll be extremely happy!

My sobriety needs to be worked on continuously and by doing this, I've just celebrated my **FIRST YEAR OF SOBRIETY** (24/05/23).

I did it and so can you.

Acknowledgements

Thank you for taking the time to read Recovery Voices. We hope it has educated, empowered, and that you felt empathy with the pieces.

All of these poems and prose were created by people who have lived experience of addiction and recovery. People who are us, could be us, have been us. People who are our neighbours, friends, fathers, sons, brothers, mothers, daughters, and sisters.

People who have been judged many times before they were able to seek help and continue to be judged whilst recovering and in their sobriety. People who have feelings, and troubles (some of which are beyond comprehension to those who have been lucky enough to not be inflicted). But they are all human, we are all human.

Thank you to the amazing, inspiring people who are involved in Recovery Connections and have contributed to this book. I have learnt something from each of you – your pieces show an insight into your mind, heart, and soul. You are all phenomenal and it has been a pleasure and honour to get an insight into your resilience, thank you.

Massive thanks to Recovery Connections staff team for wishing to embark on creating this poignant book and allowing me access to such an incredible charity and magnificent people. Special thanks to Mark Stephenson, if his belief in people could be bottled and given out, the world would be a better place. Big thanks to Dot, who saw the therapeutic creativity from this project and welcomed me with encouragement and kindness that felt like sunshine. Also thank you to Simon for your IT support, guidance, information, and help.

Thank you to all the leads in the four areas that Recovery Connections operate; Gateshead, Sunderland, Stockton, and Middlesbrough. The whole team work tirelessly to help people with a range of needs who are multiply disadvantaged. They support, believe in, and empower people to recover from substance misuse and learn how to enjoy life, instead of just existing.

Profits from this book go to Recovery Connections and Write on the Tyne – both are non-profit organisations supporting and giving opportunities to marginalised people.

If you have enjoyed this book, please leave a review on Amazon and Goodreads. Reviews help to boost the visibility of books to potential readers and also show appreciation for the story-holders and creatives involved in the many hours it takes to produce a book.

Helen Aitchison

For more information about Recovery Connections visit www.recoveryconnections.org.uk

For more information about Write on the Tyne visit www.writeonthetyne.com

Addiction Support in the UK

Alongside the following links and details, you will find a wide range of regional resources and local support networks, via search engines and directories.

Beating Addictions. Information about a range of addictive behaviours and treatments.

DrugWise. Information about drugs, alcohol and tobacco.

Change Grow Live. Information and support around alcohol and substance use.

Alcoholics Anonymous (AA). Help and support for anyone with alcohol problems.
0800 9177 650
help@aamail.org (email helpline)

SMART. Helping individuals recover from any addictive behaviour and lead meaningful & satisfying lives; using a science-based therapeutic programme of training.

Alcohol Change UK. Information and support options for people worried about how much alcohol they are drinking, in both English and Welsh.

Club Drug Clinic. Information and support for people worried about their use of recreational drugs. The clinic offers help in the London boroughs of Kensington & Chelsea, Hammersmith & Fulham and Westminster.
020 3317 3000

Cocaine Anonymous UK. Help and support for anyone who wants to stop using cocaine.
0800 612 0225
helpline@cauk.org.uk

DAN 24/7. A bilingual English and Welsh helpline for anyone in Wales in need of further information or help relating to drugs or alcohol. Also known as the Wales Drug & Alcohol Helpline.
0808 808 2234
81066 (text DAN)

Gamcare. Information and support for people who want to stop gambling, including a helpline and online forum.
0808 8020 133

Marijuana Anonymous. Help for anyone worried about cannabis use.
0300 124 0373
helpline@marijuana-anonymous.org.uk

Narcotics Anonymous. Support for anyone who wants to stop using drugs.
300 999 1212

Release. National charity that offers free and confidential advice about drugs and the law.
020 7324 2989
ask@release.org.uk (email helpline)

Sex and Love Addicts Anonymous. Support groups for people with sex and love addictions.
07984 977 884 (Infoline)

Turning Point. Health and social care services in England for people with a learning disability. Also supports people with mental health problems, drug and alcohol abuse or unemployment.

We Are With You. Supports people with drug, alcohol or mental health problems, and their friends and family.

Al-Anon. for the families & friends of people addicted to alcohol who share their experience, strength, & hope in order to solve their common problems.

Adfam. Information and support for friends and family of people with drug or alcohol problems.

Bereaved through Alcohol and Drugs (BEAD). Information and support for anyone bereaved through drug or alcohol use.

Families Anonymous. Support for friends and family of people with drug problems.
0207 4984 680

National Association for Children of Alcoholics. Provides information, advice and support for anyone affected by a parent's drinking, including adults.
0800 358 3456
helpline@nacoa.org.uk

Talk to Frank. seek information and/or advice about drugs.

Beat. UK's eating disorder charity. The National Helpline exists to encourage and empower people to get help quickly, because we know the sooner someone starts treatment, the greater their chance of recovery. People can contact them online or by phone 365 days a year.

Rape & Sexual Assault Services. Type in your postcode / local area postcode and find the closest support services to your location.

Samaritans. To talk about anything that is upsetting you, you can contact Samaritans 24 hours a day, 365 days a year. You can call 116 123 (free from any phone), email jo@samaritans.org or visit some branches in person. You can also call the Samaritans Welsh Language Line on 0808 164 0123 (7pm–11pm every day).

SANEline. If you're experiencing a mental health problem or supporting someone else, you can call SANEline on 0300 304 7000 (4.30pm–10.30pm every day).

Papyrus HOPELINEUK. If you're under 35 and struggling with suicidal feelings, or concerned about a young person who might be struggling, you can call Papyrus HOPELINEUK on 0800 068 4141 (weekdays 10am-10pm, weekends 2pm-10pm and bank holidays 2pm–10pm), email pat@papyrus-uk.org or text 07786 209 697.

Campaign Against Living Miserably (CALM). If you identify as male, you can call the Campaign Against

Living Miserably (CALM) on 0800 58 58 58 (5pm–midnight every day) or use their webchat service.

Nightline. If you're a student, you can look on the Nightline website to see if your university or college offers a night-time listening service. Nightline phone operators are all students too.

Switchboard. If you identify as gay, lesbian, bisexual or transgender, you can call Switchboard on 0300 330 0630 (10am–10pm every day), email chris@switchboard.lgbt or use their webchat service. Phone operators all identify as LGBT+.

C.A.L.L. If you live in Wales, you can call the Community Advice and Listening Line (C.A.L.L.) on 0800 132 737 (open 24/7) or you can text 'help' followed by a question to 81066.

Ask for an urgent GP appointment or call 111. 111 can tell you the right place to get help if you need to see someone. Go to 111.nhs.uk or call 111.

If you or someone you know needs immediate help, has seriously harmed themselves or is in a mental health emergency, call 999.

Printed in Poland
by Amazon Fulfillment
Poland Sp. z o.o., Wrocław

23986120R00091